THE MORMONS
by mark hedengren

All photography, including cover imagery, by Mark Hedengren

Interviews conducted by Mark Hedengren

Foreword by Robert Millet

Layout and design, including cover, by Vikki Miller

Published by Red Finch L.L.C. in the USA
www.redfinchbooks.com

Printed in Hong Kong
by Paramount Printing Company Limited

First edition

No part of this publication may be reproduced or transmitted in any form or by any means, electronic or mechanical, including photocopy or any storage and retrieval system, without permission in writing from the publisher.

All images and content © 2010 Mark Finch Hedengren

this book is dedicated to
henry and leah finch

CONTENTS

FOREWORD BY ROBERT MILLET — ix

PROCLAIMING THE GOSPEL — 01

- elder greenly — 08
- sister storm — 14
- sister lords — 22
- he si — 30
- brother bertilson — 34
- enrique — 38
- ron — 44
- sister esplin — 49
- alisa — 54
- david and jessica — 63

PERFECTING THE SAINTS — 67

- john — 70
- jessica — 77
- marie — 83
- jean-claude — 86

PERFECTING THE SAINTS (continued)

helen	95
maru	106
gösta	113
suy	114
roth	125
rebecca	129

REDEEMING THE DEAD — 139

evan	145

THE MORMONS
by mark hedengren

FOREWORD
robert millet

Mormonism is a 24/7 religion, a way of life that provides meaning and perspective for every waking (and sleeping) minute of the day. Personal life, social life, employment, recreation, study, mealtime, prayer, and even sleep—these all have spiritual roots and thus religious ramifications for Latter-day Saints. Consequently, there is not a minute of any given day that could rightly be said to be outside the pale of the religious reach. Life is religion, and religion is life. Mormons wouldn't have it any other way.

Latter-day Saints believe in what they do and who they are. They are excited about their religious persuasion and wish that all people could know what they know and feel what they feel. In that sense, they are forevermore *proclaiming the gospel*. These people believe in Jesus Christ, in his deeds of compassion, his marvelous teachings, his sacred atoning work for the salvation of all souls, and his matchless life. Imitation and emulation are among the highest forms of worship, and so Mormons strive every day to become more Christlike, both in how they conduct their personal lives and in how they love and serve others. They are always involved in *perfecting the Saints*. And finally, because members of The Church of Jesus Christ of Latter-day Saints hold to the view that life and love and learning are forever, they concern themselves not just with their brothers and sisters who now live on earth but also with those who have passed beyond the veil of death. Like their Master Jesus Christ, who had his eye fixed on eternity as well as time, they long to extend the blessings of the gospel to those who never had the sweet opportunity to know and experience the abundant life with and through Christ. Consequently, they devote a significant portion of their time to *redeeming the dead*.

In this book, *The Mormons*, Mark Hedengren, a sensitive and thoughtful photographer, has captured beautifully these three dimensions of LDS religiosity, three aspects of a people engaged in the mission of the Church of Jesus Christ. Hedengren has managed to bring life and personality to what still remains a mystery to many. Because of the power of a picture to tell a story or preach a sermon, what follows is a marvelously well-rounded and thorough presentation, an extended look at the faith and way of life of a people who deserve to be seen and heard.

Robert Millet
Abraham O. Smoot University Professor

01

mormon missionaries teaching a lesson about the book of mormon
accra, ghana

PROCLAIMING
THE GOSPEL

missionaries singing on a bus
cancun, mexico

03

baptism
cancun, mexico

04

angry missionary home in his apartment early
accra, ghana

"i fell in a ditch today. there's no kool-aid or sunny d, and i have to shower with a bucket."

05

playing the piano after a branch activity
brooklyn, new york

a missionary comforts a young mormon
managua, nicaragua

street contacting
paris, france

ELDER GREENLY
mexico merida mission
from orem, utah

Here in Mexico the family is under attack a lot. Especially here in Cancun there are a lot of problems. It's really special for me to be able to find a family, get the father excited, and get him to stop drinking (usually) and realize the important role that he has as a patriarch of his home. Sometimes we succeed and we get a family that changes and gets out of the cycle of drunkenness or poverty, and they get into the loop of the Church and prosperity; that really makes me happy. It is really important to me because I love my Father in Heaven and Jesus Christ.

Meeting people is not really the same every day. We usually walk around and talk to people all day. We find out what they do and what makes them happy. You can kind of see what has and hasn't gone right for others and from that you can understand what you can do as a father one day when it is your turn. It's great to be able to know people and to be able to bring them to Christ so they can know about the gospel truths and be able to return to Heavenly Father with their families.

Four months into my mission, they asked me to be a trainer, and I didn't really know how to do that. I'm a cheerful, smiley kind of guy. I like to have fun. My companion is more serious. He is a chemist. So we had a lot of different problems with how we were and what kind of things we liked. We were just really different.

We were sent to open up a new village of three thousand people that had been shut down for three years. We were kind of overwhelmed with what we had been called to do. We got along great, but sometimes we would fight. You know how it is. Even though we were so different, the hand of the Lord was seen in that village. When we started, there were maybe six going to church, and one week before we left, there was a peak of ninety-seven people, which shows that the Lord really strengthened us and we were able to help that village to get back where it needed to be.

Every day there is something I learn that I can use. You know how it is—you're a missionary. The ability to look at other families and see what happens with them: what they do well and what they do wrong. Just the other day I met a woman that had a Mormon neighbor a few years ago that kicked her out of her house, destroyed her photographs, and did some evil stuff to her, and she said, "I don't have any desire to listen to you at all." And I thought, "What if that neighbor had loved that woman and fellowshipped her? The Church would have a strong member because she knew the Bible well." We had the opportunity to really serve and serve well, but this woman wasn't able to accept the gospel because of what her neighbor had done. Those are the kind of insights that I learn daily, and I know they will help me one day to be a righteous dad and a good husband and help out my family in whatever way I can.

It's hard sometimes to have to pick up and leave it all because I like where I am, I know the people and my companion. They tell us about our transfer at night—six o'clock the next morning we have to be on the bus. We have twelve hours to pack and go, and that has always been a little hard for me personally—to just have to pick up and leave all your friends and experiences. You leave, and you trust in the Lord that you did something well and that the people you helped will be trained.

I like to leave families that are united again, without any alcohol abuse, without any spouse abuse, without any major problems—a family that is united in the gospel. Even if I leave only one family, that's fine. You know, there are a lot of people that I've been able to help and that I've seen be baptized, but as we all know, sometimes that special family really fights for it and achieves that love. Personally, this is what I want from my mission. That's the greatest spiritual high that I can live for.

09

elder greenly and his companion in a mormon chapel under construction
cancun, mexico

missionary choir singing at temple square
salt lake city, utah

missionaries talking before a district meeting
glasgow, scotland

sister storm greets a child on temple square
salt lake city temple square mission

SISTER STORM
salt lake city temple square mission
from california

My whole life I wanted to serve a mission. I have two older sisters that have both served missions. When I was in fourth grade, my oldest sister decided to serve. It was something my parents have always encouraged, and it's just been in the plans for me. You go to college, you go on a mission, then you get married—whenever that happens. And so I didn't have to think about it. I just went. But before I went there were a few obstacles. I had my papers and something came up; I didn't want to go anymore because I was twenty-one and my life was perfect. I was going to college. I had good friends. I loved my life and I didn't want to give that up. I had a cell phone. I had a car. I could take naps whenever I wanted to. And so I didn't want to serve a mission because I'd have to give up all that. I didn't want to go. I delayed for about six months, but the whole time I knew I had to go. When those obstacles cleared up, I went on my mission. It is something I always wanted to do, something I always knew was just in the plan for me, because my life has always been very structured: you go to high school, then college, then mission. There's no other option; it's just one of those steps I had to accomplish, that I knew I had to do.

Between six and nine months of being out, Temple Square sisters usually get sent to a proselyting mission for a while, for the experience. I went out to Minnesota when I was about a year out, which is not very typical. There weren't any new sisters coming from the MTC, and you need at least 150 sisters on Temple Square or 130 to have it function. Typically you have 150 and we weren't getting any from the MTC, and people kept on leaving. So we had to keep sisters here. I went to Minnesota, and I think the biggest difference was you didn't teach as much. And that is the whole reason why you want to serve a mission, is to teach people about the gospel. You didn't see people very often. We would tract around four hours a day, every single day in knee-high snow in negative-15-degree weather—you know, typical missionary stories.

But I loved it because that's what I dreamed my mission would be. And so we would get in maybe two doors a week, and we would teach maybe three lessons a week. That was the hardest thing, and that was the biggest difference. That was probably the only difference besides the amount of downtime—tracting and riding to places, like going to appointments and going to members' homes for dinner, and going to three hours of church or to family home evening or different activities—that was not available on Temple Square. So there is a lot of downtime. But it was still missionary work, just more relaxed. On Sunday at Temple Square all the sister missionaries meet at 7 o'clock in the morning for an hour for sacrament meeting. I arrived at Temple Square on December 15. And so it was crazy. Christmas time is fun because you are working a lot, but it's very, very stressful and hectic. Just like conference.

They prepare you. They get you all hyped up for it, and they have meetings to get you spiritually ready and to really focus you on what's important. Because sometimes you can think about the numbers too much (as missionaries tend to do), but it's about the people. The only time that members come to Temple Square is during Christmas and conference, so it's a totally different kind of missionary work because you are trying to help others with their missionary work. It's very fun, it's very stressful, it's very tiring. It's also very frustrating because members of the Church generally don't want to do missionary work, and so it's hard to get them refocused on that. And that is basically what your mission is: to help other people with their missionary work.

During the summer especially, there are motor coaches that come. And motor coaches could have from 20 people to 150, and you get to take them on tours, but generally you just get a lot of tourists that come and you try to figure out where their background is and just try to initiate and tell them about the Church—and as quickly as possible.

interview with sister storm
salt lake city temple square mission

You basically get to teach them the first lesson about the Restoration; you teach them what the Church is about, what the Book of Mormon is, how it is the literal restoration of Jesus Christ's Church. You just teach them the basic principles.

The biggest question we are asked would probably be, What makes your church different from any other church? I say, it's the same church that Jesus Christ organized. We have prophets. We have temples, which bind our families together forever. We have the Book of Mormon, which is a record of people living in the ancient Americas. The basic principles are that we have prophets and that Jesus Christ is the head of this church and it is his church.

Having so many sisters around can be very challenging. When I got my call to Temple Square, I was devastated, absolutely devastated. One of the reasons why is because I didn't have any girlfriends. They were too much maintenance, too much drama, too sensitive, and I didn't want to deal with that. Going to Temple Square, I wondered how I would deal with 150 girls. But it is so surprising, there is hardly any drama. If there was drama, I didn't see it. And most of the sisters are the same way that I am. They didn't have any girlfriends before or they hate drama. It was the best part about Temple Square—creating those friendships with sisters from all around the world.

Every six weeks you change companions. We have sisters from all around the world, and you have to be with just them all the time— you give tours with them, you teach with them, just like any other companionship except you switch every six weeks.

A growing experience? OK. Well, I'll be honest with you—I did not like Temple Square when I first got there. My whole life I dreamed of trudging through jungles or going tracting in Oklahoma. It was what I pictured missionary work to be: going to people inside their homes, teaching them, building relationships, and going to family wards, and getting to know the members, and helping them with their missionary work. Everything I dreamed missionary work was, Temple Square wiped out. It was what the Lord wanted me to do, and so I was willing to do that. And at the time I said, OK, I'll do it. But I wasn't happy about it. So I went, and I had a very pessimistic attitude, and I didn't realize it. I would say to myself, "It is not my fault; it's just because I'm here in Temple Square. When I get to go out into the field or proselyting, I'll be happy because that is my mission. And this is not my mission. This is not where I'm supposed to be." Really, though, I knew I was supposed to be there.

Around six months into my mission, I realized how amazing Temple Square really was. I was able to teach, and it exemplified all the skills and talents that I had. And it was the perfect mission for me. The first thing I said, after fifteen minutes of crying, when I got my mission call was, "I don't want to harass members for referrals." That's what I thought Temple Square sisters did, because whenever I go there they would always ask me who I knew that would want to hear the gospel. I didn't want to be that kind of missionary, harassing members for referrals. I had no idea what really went on in Temple Square and what a sacred place it really was.

After I realized that it had become a habit for me to hate Temple Square, I started changing my thoughts. I would decide not to say anything negative about Temple Square. As I stopped saying things, I started thinking less negative thoughts, and I learned to love it. By the time I went to Minnesota, I didn't want to go because I loved everything about it. That was a life lesson: I learned that you can be happy in whatever situation you are in and that Heavenly Father wants you to be happy, and he gives you things for your happiness.

That was a growing experience: not liking Temple Square and being totally disappointed with my dreams and aspirations of what missionary work is supposed to be and then realizing that the Lord gives you what you need for you to be the best and for you to be the happiest. There are lots of good stories that happen on Temple Square because you meet people all the time. Sometimes you meet those people who are prepared, and they are like, "Wow, this is what I've been looking for. Tell me more. I want to learn more." We then send the missionaries to them, and we never find out what happens. We just pray that the missionaries visit them and that they will still continue to have a willing heart once they leave Temple Square and leave the spirit on Temple Square. Those experiences happen all the time. You meet people and you teach them. You see them change. You see the light in their eyes. But those experiences really didn't have much of an impact on me compared to the casual encounters that you have where you specifically make a difference, where your personality and the experiences that you have had in your life alter the way a person feels about himself, or alter how they feel about God, or alter how they feel about life in general. They may not want the missionaries or anything, but if you made a positive influence in their life, that's what missionary work is all about for me. When I would meet those people, a lot of them didn't want to talk to the missionaries, but I knew that I was specifically there for them, that the experiences in my life were in some way related to helping and empathizing with those people specifically.

interview with sister storm
salt lake city temple square mission

There was one time I met this father and his son. I was at a gate assignment, on south gate. (As you enter, the sisters are always standing right there.) We were late for another assignment, so we weren't going to go to the south gate, but we just went for the five minutes we had before we had to be at the next place. While we were there they came in, and they started asking us questions. I give them a map, and I start explaining where things are, where they can go, and we start answering all the usual questions like, What makes your church different from any other church? So we talked to them about families because he is with his son, and you could see that they had a really good bond. We started teaching about families and temples and why we have temples and how our families can be bound forever. You could literally see the change. Our personalities had clicked instantly. We left them with an idea of where they could eat and what tours they could take.

The next day, we were taking a tour and we were running late, we weren't supposed to be in this area which we were in, and the same father and son walked in. We saw each other, and I didn't remember them because it happens all the time—you make those contacts all the time with people. They remembered me, and they came up to me, and they were really excited to see me. But I had to be at another assignment, so I brought them with me to the Beehive House, which is Brigham Young's first home. I took them on a tour there, and I taught them all about families and the Book of Mormon. At the end of that tour, we spent about an hour just teaching them. They were so excited, and they wanted that in their life. And I felt so excited about that because I knew it was because of my personality and the Lord putting me in the right place at the right time. I was thankful; I mean, it was nothing that I did. It was just the Lord using what he has given me. I don't know what happened to them. You know, I sent the missionaries to their home, and that is all I know.

On Temple Square the hard thing is that you are making a constant first impression. It is so exhausting. Every single person you meet, their impression of you is their impression of the Church. So no matter how bad you are feeling, no matter how sick you are, no matter how tired you are or how mad you are, no matter what feeling you have, you have to be happy because that is what the gospel is about. It was so hard not to be genuine on Temple Square and for those six months when I was being negative, it was exhausting faking the happiness. Once I caught the glimpse of the gift that I had been given of how to be happy in any situation, that is when it became so enjoyable and when I became truly happy, and I wasn't faking it anymore. And so the tragedy of my mission is those six wasted months of faking happiness. I wasn't appreciating what Heavenly Father had given me because he had given me something so great, but I didn't see it for what it was.

There are stalkers that come and visit you all the time and are creepy, and you have to call security and things like that. There are people that come to try to save us, friends of other faiths, and I always love them. I seriously did because I appreciated them coming to share their faith with me, and that they would care for me that much to try to save me. They would come on our tours, they would come on bus loads of youth groups, and they ask very deep questions and very Bible bashing questions. We would have a tour group of twenty people, and if two of them were being harassing, we would have to ask them to leave or tell them that we would answer their questions between stops. They didn't want answers; they just wanted to make everyone else on the tour think, or bring a negative feeling to the tour. They would tape-record us sometimes, and we would have to get security, and they would basically just try to get us angry. I would just ask them if they would like missionaries to visit them to answer their questions, and of course they didn't, so they would leave.

I didn't Bible-bash, but I tried to answer questions as best as possible, and you always get to a point where you have to agree to disagree. But that is not the point of the gospel; the point is to make everyone feel loved because that is what the gospel is all about—Heavenly Father loves you so much that he has given you all these things. He has given you prophets. He has given you a temple. He has given you priesthood authority. He has given you the Book of Mormon. He has given you everything. And so for them to walk away because of a disagreement on a translation of the Bible, it's not the point. So you just kindly let them know that you love them.

I thought I would be a different person on my mission; premission Lindsay liked to have fun and went to school. When I came on my mission, I didn't know how Sister Storm was supposed to act. There was a time period when I just wanted to be exactly like the person training me, and it's then hard to integrate your personality into the work. Once you figure that out, missionary work becomes so much better.

Then coming home from your mission, you have to figure out and live through another identity crisis because you start asking, "Who am I?" and "Who is returned-missionary Lindsay?" I know who Sister Storm is. I don't want to be premission Lindsay, but I need to know who I am. And so the big difference I see is perspective on life and having more

interview with sister storm
salt lake city temple square mission

motivation to do what is right. I've always asked returned missionaries what they learned most. For me it's perspective on what's really important in life. It's kind of blurry sometimes, but I know what is right, and I know how to live the gospel now.

My goal was to love my mission, and I did that. I loved it so much that the night before I went home I bawled like crazy. When you first get on your mission, it seems like a dream, and you can only think about real life. But once you are on your mission, real life becomes a dream and this is your life. When you get off your mission, it seems like a dream that you even served a mission.

I remember walking off the plane, and I saw my mom and I just started bawling. Not because I was happy to see her, but because I realized that the happiest point of my life this far was over. It was the happiest, and it was the hardest by far, but it was over, and I will never be able to go back to that point in my life. It was a really hard adjustment at first getting back into the swing of things with people expecting you to be normal, but knowing that you are going to have an adjustment period but not understanding why it's so hard. I cried for a few days, but I feel like I'm adjusting pretty well.

It's still hard because life is so distracting, and it becomes difficult to live the basic principles of the gospel. On your mission, though, you don't think how hard it is. It is just easy. But when you get back, you have to go to class, you have friends, you have family, you have all these things you have to do in a day, and the gospel gets pushed aside. And so you go through adjustment periods trying to figure out how to live the gospel in real life, and that's hard, really hard.

I felt really awkward in social situations because when you talk to people on your mission, you are always thinking, "How can I apply this to the gospel?" or "How can I integrate the gospel into this conversation?" When you get back, people don't want that, and it's weird if you do that. And you do it for a while, and people think you are strange, and so I didn't want to be social—I wanted to go and read. I didn't want to be here because it seemed pointless and a waste of time.

I try to be genuine about my mission. It was the best time of my life, but I did not like my mission for six months, and that's a long time. I'm embarrassed to say that. But it's the truth. Returned missionaries always talk about how much they want to go back. I loved it, but I know that I'm in the right place at the right time now, and that's what life is about—being in the right place at the right time and figuring out what you are supposed to do that is going to make you happy. So as much as I loved that time in my life, I wouldn't want to go back to it. I would want to serve another mission, dozens, but not that one, because those lessons were learned, and by the end of the mission I felt I had completed what I was supposed to do.

The mission president I had for the majority of my time serving in the Temple Square mission was very like a grandpa. He was just there for us all the time. He was the president of 150 sisters so he spent most of his time in his office and always had sisters outside his door in tears waiting to see him. That's what makes the sisters so good—we are compassionate and emotional, but that is actually really tiring for the mission president. So he was just there, constantly working with the missionaries; he had the mission under tight supervision.

Millions of people come to Temple Square every year, and we have to make a good impression, it's like we are the eye of the Church. It's the best feeling though, having that responsibility.

I love it when missionaries come back and tell us a referral from Temple Square helped. I love it. That's the most rewarding feeling, and those are my success stories.

missionaries present in front of the *christus* statue at temple square
salt lake city, utah

missionary schedules an appointment with an anti-mormon protestor
salt lake city, utah

former missionary companions greet each other at a meeting
stockholm, sweden

missionaries pray before they leave to go teach
barcelona, spain

SISTER LORDS
ghana, west africa
from utah

sister lords is escorted from an investigator's house
cape coast, ghana

I expected when we got here that Africa would be dry and all brown. But when we got here, it's all green and beautiful. It's got trees and all kinds of vegetation, and it's just gorgeous.

Well, we have people come looking for us, like Samuel. We were teaching in Foso or Praaso, and a man came looking for us, and he said that he had a group that wanted to listen to lessons, and that was where we were today in Hermoni and Kurmani. And he asked if we'd come out and teach them. It started with one group, and it's become bigger and bigger, and he just told me today he wants to convert half the village. That's his goal.

One of the things I think is hard is that people will come up to you and ask you to buy them certain things, or they want money. And it's hard because we have done a lot to help them.

I love working with people. I love children and families. That's what's been hard for me—I want to do everything for everybody. But you can't because everybody has needs, lots of needs, but we do what we can to help them. When people have asked, we've helped them.

Africa is a lot different from home. At home you have all the conveniences. Supermarkets and grocery stores? Yes. But things like restaurants and fast-food places, they just aren't here. You're not going to find them here in Ghana. But we've discovered since we've been here that you can find just about anything if you know where to look or if someone can tell you. Like in Praaso we found that you can buy just about anything. But when we first got here, we didn't think we could get anything that we were used to.

I did social work before we left, and I really think that it has helped a lot, for me anyway, because I can get the kids, and my husband loves to play with the kids. You should see the way the kids play with him. Once he's out there, he's just surrounded by them. He goes out, and they just run around him.

Before we got our call, we were still working full-time jobs—both of us. And so we both had to retire. So we retired right as we left, and then we came here, to Ghana. So when we go home, we are going to say, "What are we going to do now?"

missionaries in front of a mormon church
cancun, mexico

a missionary gets a package from home
stockholm, sweden

a missionary studies the scriptures
barcelona, spain

missionaries shopping for ties
new york, new york

he si, who converted to the church of jesus christ of latter-day saints while studying in sweden
stockholm, sweden

HE SI
shanghai, china
convert to the church

It was my birthday when I first learned about the Church. My friend brought two missionaries to my party, and before it started they talked to me about the Church. This is the first time I had heard about it, although I did have some knowledge about the Christian church and Jesus Christ before so I was a little bit interested. I told them that they could come to visit me more.

After that they would usually come about once a week, and they would have a new theme every time. They told me about repentance, and they started at the basics, telling me everything I needed to know. Sometimes we discussed some really interesting topics that were in several chapters of the Book of Mormon. They would show me which they thought were the best chapters, and we would share our thoughts on them together.

As time went by, I learned more about the Church, but I realized if I wanted to know more I would have to learn about the people that go to church, and the best thing to do is to go to meetings and meet people. I come to the Sunday meetings every week and I find that I learn more from the talks and lessons every week. I have learned many more things. I've learned about the reason for living, and that is an enrichment to me. What I have learned is limited, but through reading and coming to church I can absorb more knowledge.

First, if we want to learn English more, we can learn by reading the Bible. It is one of the sources from which we learn English. My cousin is a Christian herself, so sometimes when we meet I have many things to ask her because I am so curious, and she tells me.

Once we watched a movie about Joseph Smith. I was kind of moved by that movie because when he was so young, like me, he made up his mind to come close to God and pray, and he got an answer. My first impression was that I really have to devote myself to something that I want. One of the important things that I want is to come close to God, so I should do things more like the way Joseph Smith did them. The Church teaches no drinking and to leave all the addictive habits alone and repent. There is also the importance of family mentioned, and these things touched me because as a Chinese I love my family very much, and they supported my decision to come to Sweden to study. I like that I can pray for them and everyone I care about.

At first my family were skeptical about the Church. It's not that they didn't like it—they just knew very little about the Mormon Church, so they just told me that I had to get to know it all first before I made any huge decisions. I think they did some research on the Internet about the Mormon Church, and they found things that were good, and they discovered that it's a good thing to be able to get baptized, because Sweden is more open than China. They now think it's good, and they've changed their attitude and have become more supportive.

My dad was all right, and my mum was a little concerned because there are some movements about religion in China that have not turned out very well because they become so obsessed with religion, and some of them do some crazy things. So what I did was I told them every week what we talked about in the meetings and what we did and what I learned. I wanted them to know that all of these things are helping me to grow up spiritually. It's not an obsession or something extreme, and it's now good for my mum to embrace the fact that I am going to church.

Sometimes when I feel depressed, maybe because of studies at school or something, I start thinking about what I learned at church, or I read the Book of Mormon or read some inspiring talks given at general conference. It always helps me change my mind for the better, and it gives me the push I need to keep going.

the bertilson family studies scriptures together during family home evening
handen, sweden

BROTHER BERTILSON
handen, sweden
convert to the church

I first properly heard about the Church when I came to Brigham Young University. Of course, before that, I had heard something in school, in religion class about something or someone called the Mormons, but I had no real idea what it was. I was finishing my military service here in Sweden, and I got a letter from BYU, where they invited me to come and join the track team and have a scholarship. I was very pleased by their offer and very much interested to go there because I had always had a dream of coming to the United States and going to Disneyland. Actually, that is why I was interested in going there, to get a chance to see Disneyland, a longtime wish or dream.

When I got this scholarship, I saw the opportunity to go to Disneyland. I looked up where BYU and Provo were, so I wasn't too far away from Disneyland in Los Angeles. So that was the first idea.

The letterhead did not say The Church of Jesus Christ of Latter-day Saints, as I recall. I never looked at that.

However, I had to work. I had to finish my military service, and I had to work for half a year because the plane ticket wasn't included. So I got there without knowing that this Brigham Young University was part of the Church. I had not noticed that. I was unaware. I had just got the ticket, and I went there.

So I came, and I was unpacking. I had a very nice roommate, Tim Kennedy, who met me and introduced me to the dormitories, Helaman Halls. And I was very impressed by him and his kind manners. And in the evening, I was unpacking, and I saw these other boys. They were playing and listening to the radio. Then someone whistled in the lobby, and I can still feel the reverence, or rather, I was impressed but confused. All the boys, as I saw it, left their things and went to the lobby. Tim came to me and said, "Bo, come." I didn't know what to do, but he said, "Come."

I went with him to this lobby, and there were maybe fifty to one hundred boys. One of them stood on a chair, and he gave a short talk. I don't remember what he said. This gathering was, of course, repeated daily. It was an evening fireside, and it was a very short thing, maybe just a few minutes. But anyway, I was impressed by the reverence shown by the other boys. When I had been in the military (I was a sergeant) I would call the other soldiers and try to get them to gather, and it was not that easy. But here they all came on their own without a repeated command. And they also stood there and just listened to this young man.

So I was really wondering, "What is this?" And he was quoting some prophet or wise man or something like that. And then after these minutes of thoughts, all the boys fell on their knees, and I just stood there wondering, "What is this?" I had never been in a situation similar to that, and I'm sure they did not know that I was not a member. Tim didn't know, obviously. Or maybe he did. I don't know. I've never asked him. But, anyway, they were all waiting for something, and it took me I don't know how many seconds to understand that they were waiting for me. I was in the midst of all these boys. I had no escape. I didn't want to escape, it was just something very strange to me. So I fell on my knees too.

Then this was my first experience with what I believe was the Spirit. I felt a very strong warm feeling while one of the other boys said the evening prayer. And from then on, I knew that this was not a regular university.

I very soon found out, of course, there were codes. On the first Sunday I noticed everyone was going to church. They dressed up. And I had no nice clothes. I never had that. Well, my mom was always keen on us having nice clothes and clean clothes, but I had no Sunday clothes,

interview with brother bertilson
handen, sweden

so to say. I was amazed, and I was very much pleased by seeing that they were honest, they were the people as I saw them. They were thrifty. They liked to work. Most of the students had to work, and they were practicing their talents. They were either on the ballet team, track team, or musical talent team. So, I really thought, this is a wonderful place. I really liked it.

And, of course, after a few weeks I got interested in going to church with them. I would usually use my Sundays to work out, train, and have really long runs. Then someone invited me to go to church. So I went, and I found out that they were having church meetings in classrooms, which was also a little bit odd for me.

But I really liked the things I heard because they were speaking on daily subjects: practical daily religion. So I liked that too. And, of course, after that, there were roommates and others that invited me to listen to the missionaries. And I was a little bit hesitant because I was in a foreign country and I had no religion. Well, I had been confirmed here in Sweden in my youth, thirteen or fourteen years of age, so I had some. I had studied the Bible of course. It was a hard time for me to get into the Joseph Smith story and church because it wasn't that obvious for me to just accept it all, even though the thing that made me want to listen was the lifestyle of the members and my roommates. They really lived the lifestyle that I liked and had actually lived very close to. I was never prone to use drugs. I didn't drink coffee. The only thing I really had to change in my life was to stop drinking tea. That was the only thing. I also had no girlfriends. I had never had anything like that in my life. So it was not hard. It was something that I really wanted to know.

I listened to the missionaries, yes. My training course was to run up the mountains. I had a place way up where I used to kneel down and ask God to answer my prayers. I prayed for a testimony of not only God, because that was the first thing I needed, but a testimony of the power he has to answer prayers. After I got that answer, the next step was to ask God if this church was true, if it was restored, if the Book of Mormon was true, if Joseph Smith was a prophet, and if we have new prophets today. So it was a constant thing—I used my running to pray. Every day I was up in the mountains, and I really grew a desire to plant the seed. I was, of course, reading the Book of Mormon; it was the scriptures that helped me to understand how a testimony can be planted and how you can feel what is right. And I did have that experience of the seed that was planted and that was growing. So the day came within a few months that I really felt that this was what

I wanted to embrace. By then I had started to go to church every Sunday and I had stopped working and running on Sunday. I had also started being a home teacher even before I was a member.

I had a wonderful quorum president, and he was excellent in taking care of me and taking interviews after home teaching visits. I had many other good friends in my church family. They were a great part of my feeling good there. There was a girl that was especially welcoming. Not just one, but one that should be mentioned. It was Susan Brown. At the first ward activity she came and invited me to dance, and I had never actually been a dancer. I think I had only been at one dance before that, and I was very shy. But she helped me overcome my shyness, well not overcome, but she helped me to understand there was no fear.

Anyway, my branch president, when I actually talked to him, I said I wanted to get baptized. He said, "I feel you should talk to your parents first," even though I was twenty years old. So I called home. I remember my dad said, "Well, are you sure you know what to do?" They, by then, had read my letters, so they knew that I was kind of investigating the Church and that the Church was very present at this university. And he said, "Well, I know you have always made good choices, so I trust you will do this now too." My mom, she said, "I had the feeling this was coming." She also expressed her concerns. So I decided to wait to get baptized and visit Stockholm first. When I got home I met two nice elders, Elder Croft and Elder Neilson. They were very kind, and had, of course, gotten my name as a reference from Utah. So they came and they continued the teaching, and the date was set and I was baptized.

My focus and goals changed. When I went to BYU, I first wanted to be an Olympic runner—I wanted to run for Sweden in 1980. I was also studying to be a medical doctor. I still had that goal when I became a member, but I decided to try the Lord's path and I followed his commandments and went where it led me. That is what I promised when I was baptized: that I would try the Lord's way, and I have not strayed from that. I have kept my part of the promise.

My priorities changed significantly. Running became my fourth priority, and that's how it ended. I never got to the Olympics in Moscow, but I got something much better. I got my wife, Nancy. And I got my family—we have six children. I'm even a grandfather now, and we are all very good, strong individuals.

the bertilson family kneels to pray
handen, sweden

ENRIQUE
barcelona, spain
convert to the church

I met the missionaries in front of this building in the street, while I was crossing to enter in the university. I stopped to talk with them and they showed me a pamphlet and a picture of the apostles. They told me about the Church, and they had a great message to share with me. I was surprised because they were nineteen years old, and I could talk with them about a lot of things I had been looking for.

Then we met in the church in Plaza del Centro here in Barcelona. This was the first chapel of the Church in the city, and they had the institute of religion. We met there to have the classes with them. And they told me a lot of new things. And one of the best was the work we can do in temples for our ancestors, because I had a special feeling about my father, who died in 2001. And what I felt is that I had to do something to help him, that I could do something that was good for him. And one of the missionaries, Alan Brennan, he was called, he told me about the work we can do in the temples. It was marvelous to know this. I felt something, especially in my mind, a clear vision of the truth of this.

Then I was always surprised, because I felt so natural about the message, about the lessons, about the gospel. And I remembered the first time I met them in the street and I had the feeling of recognizing them. When I met them, it was April 13, 2005, and when I continued hearing about the Restoration of the gospel and the other things they taught me, they asked me if I would be baptized. Naturally I said yes. And this was the best choice I made in my life. I have discovered a lot of new things I didn't know. But the best is that I was a happy person when I met the missionaries, and now I know about happiness and truth. And I have received a testimony from the Spirit on many occasions.

One of my best experiences was when I helped the missionaries teach the lessons to two young people from Cameroon. They could only speak French. I lived in France for two years when I was five and six years old. I didn't use French anymore, but at this time the missionaries asked for my languages and gifts so I could learn French in three weeks and talk about all the lessons in French for these young boys. And then they came to the church and were baptized. Now they are in other places in Spain looking for work and places to live. And they are my friends; they are very good friends of mine. They were living with me for six months, and I had a great experience because they were from another culture, another language, another country, but we had a very good relationship living together.

To be a companion of the missionaries and their work is a very stimulating activity. And I love all things in the Church. I love a lot of the old people, and I love those who are working for the gospel to have it be known in every part of the world. And this is what I was looking for with no knowledge about it. I felt it before I had anything to do with the Church. I felt like a priest, but I was sure I didn't want to be a priest of the Catholic Church. Now I have discovered what the priesthood really is, and I am so grateful for the trust of God in me to have the priesthood and to help others to have the blessings of God. It is a great experience to be there with the people who need the help of God.

Before I met the missionaries, I always felt there was a large period of gospel history missing, because I have read the New Testament, but I knew this was two thousand years old, and we have new problems for these times. So shouldn't there be something that is helping us live God's lessons and teachings? And when I found the missionaries and I saw the photographs of the apostles and the prophet, it was a nice thing to know they were here.

enrique, a doctoral student in philosophy who converted to the church of jesus christ of latter-day saints
barcelona, spain

missionaries practice street contacting at a regional meeting
stockholm, sweden

missionaries wash their laundry and write letters to their families
new york, new york

a missionary explains the book of mormon
cancun, mexico

missionaries recite scriptures before a district meeting
glasgow, scotland

RON
moab, utah
convert to the church

Well, I had a friend. He was a member of the Church. He was older than I was, and we went to high school together. We worked together at a newspaper in Escondido, California, and he had talked a lot about the Church. But I just knew he was different from the rest of us. He used to hang around and tell jokes, you know, just horse around. He was a little different. I guess I always remembered that. Then I became a little familiar with his brother and his sister and other members of his family. So they were the only members of the Church that I had around. He went on to become a bishop and the stake president and regional representative. He has been a mission president and temple president, and I wouldn't be surprised if he isn't a General Authority one of these days. But I will always remember him, his example, I guess.

So when I met Pat, she was also a member of the Church. I think the time came in my life that I was ready for change, ready for a change in my life. So that's when I became interested in the Church.

Well, I had to quit smoking. I never was a drinker. I drank some, but I wasn't a happy drinker. But I quit smoking. I quit, and it was actually harder than when I had tried to quit before. I found it to be almost impossible. But when I met the missionaries and a ward missionary, who taught me several times, they said the whole ward and all the missionaries and everybody were going to fast and pray for me. And so actually that's when I quit, at that time. It was actually easier. It was an easy thing with all the fasting and praying going on for me. But it wasn't easy before. I tried numerous times and couldn't quit, so I guess quitting smoking was the hardest thing probably for me, except it turned out it wasn't all that hard.

The Church has changed my life. Well, I don't know if it has changed it. I don't know where I'd be now if it wasn't for the Church. But it has not only influenced my life, but my whole family's life. You know, we moved here (Utah) about thirty years ago almost, to get out of California and to go back into a small community like I was raised in. But all of our kids are successful kids, and they are good kids. They haven't been involved in drugs or bad influences. So I attribute that to the Church.

I have three kids, a boy and two daughters. My son served a mission in Puerto Rico, and he is married with children. My two daughters, one is a member of the sheriff's department in Moab; my other daughter, she's in the Relief Society presidency.

It's neat. It's fun. I enjoy it.

ron in a mormon church building
moab, utah

a family prepares for a final photograph before their son enters the MTC
Provo, Utah

sister esplin and her companion talk to two young men in a shopping center
farsta, sweden

SISTER ESPLIN
farsta, sweden
from salt lake city, utah

My name is Sister Esplin, and I'm a missionary. I'm on a mission because I have a testimony that this is the one true church. And I know that by sharing this message with others I can bring happiness into their lives.

I feel like there are people out there that I need to teach, that are waiting for me to bring them the gospel. And even if there is just one person, I feel like I can make a difference. I heard that Sweden was really hard when I got my calling, but I really felt like there was that one person whose life I was supposed to help. And that is what motivates me to be here.

I know I've changed a lot by just being out in the field for one month and being in the MTC for two months. My perspective on a lot of the aspects of missionary work has changed, and I think there has been a lot of change in myself as well. Missionary work requires patience and humility, and I think that will definitely prepare me for the world when I return—in how I deal with people, how I will raise my family, and how I will be a better missionary for my friends and family.

When I meet someone who doesn't have a belief in God, it really makes me sad that they do not recognize the love that God has for them. You talk to them, and they don't really care about what happens after life or what happens in their life now. I think talking to those people is really hard because you bear your testimony and you tell them the truth about the Church and about the restored gospel, and they don't want to listen. It's hard when people don't want to listen.

The best part of missionary work is when you find someone that wants to hear more and they are excited about reading the scriptures and learning about the gospel and you watch them make steps towards the light. What's important to me is making a difference.

senior missionaries talk with sister esplin during a soccer game
stockholm, sweden

alisa rides the subway
new york, new york

ALISA
new york, new york
convert to the church

I read *The God Makers* in June, and then over the summer was when I was anti-Mormon. And then in September, I was homesick, lying in bed. There was a Book of Mormon on the top shelf of my sister's closet. I thought, "I'm going to go read it. I'm going to read it so I can map it—*The God Makers* and the Book of Mormon—and prove the Book of Mormon wrong." I knew I couldn't just go off the book *The God Makers*. I needed to read what *The God Makers* was talking about, you know, to know if it was true or not. But I actually started out with the intent to substantiate *The God Makers* and prove the Book of Mormon wrong. I started reading it, and I had my little notebook out, and literally within the first three chapters, I put the notebook down and then I just read the Book of Mormon all the way through, all in that week, probably because I was sick, really sick, so I was home in bed.

It kind of freaked me out after reading it, because I knew *The God Makers* was totally just a piece of trash.

I had mentioned in passing that I read the Book of Mormon. So my friend got all excited, and she invited me to some discussions. The first discussion I went to, my sister was home, and she decided she was going to come with me, to make sure she clarified everything. She was anti. So the first couple of discussions didn't go very well, and then it ended. This was probably like November-ish of my junior year. The discussions ended by Christmas.

I got chosen to go to girls' state the next summer too. I get to girls' state and, lo and behold, my two roommates are Mormon, and we start talking a lot. And I had brought a Book of Mormon with me, and as soon as I got back I wanted to start taking discussions. I started taking discussions, and it went very fast because by then, it's like I had a testimony. There was no like bolt of "yes this is true." It was just over time—it was just like something I just instinctively knew to be true, and I was feeding off it, even though I didn't realize it at the time. I look back, and I think of how much I read, not just the Book of Mormon; I read *Jesus the Christ,* and I read—not the *Journal of Discourses,* that came later—but I was reading like everything, studying the history of the Church too.

At this point, my parents were very stressed out, because all they knew about the Church was whisperings and weird things. And the saving grace in this was that they did have these very good friends from when we were in England—my parents have always been good friends with those people—and one family in particular, the Calls, were Mormons. My mom would call up Sherri Call, whose husband, Bill, was a bishop at the time in Texas, and she would have nightly discussions with her. My mom felt like the Mormons were not going to tell the truth and that they would try and deceive people, but because she and Sherri had been friends for fifteen years she felt she could trust her. If she had a tough question to ask her, she knew Sherri was going to answer it.

And I think that helped a lot to dispel some of the gross inaccuracies that they had heard. They finally got to a point, after much angst and arguing, where they said, "OK, just at least wait until you are eighteen."

And I said OK. But then came June, and I was just like, "No, I'm not going to wait until I'm eighteen, I'm not going to wait till December, I want to get baptized now." But, before my baptism, there had been all this angst, and there was a period that we didn't even talk about it; it was off the table.

When someone finds out that a kid is going to get baptized in the Mormon Church, everyone knows, and so all these people had been calling my mom, you know, informing her about the "truth" of the Church. I think at this point, they kind of came to terms—"Well, this

interview with alisa
new york, new york

is her choice"—but then they get all these phone calls and people are like, "Well, you need to take her to see this man. He is an ex-Mormon bishop, and he is an authority. He will be able to, you know, explain to you everything that the missionaries may not have fully divulged."

My mom honestly thought this is a legitimate thing. So she tells me about it, and I agreed, I said OK, because I was kind of cocky, and I was kind of like, "Bring it on." We go up to Sacramento the day before. I can't remember the guy's name, but I remember we walk into his office and there is a bunch of people in there and they have maps on the walls, with diagrams, with pins in them showing the Mormon population all over the world. We go into his back office, and his walls are lined with the Book of Mormon, *Jesus the Christ*, *Journal of Discourses*, just like tons of books. So we sat down at this long table—he is a big man with a long beard and glasses, and he spits when he talks.

I don't think he was expecting me to know that much. And he explained he had written *The God Makers* and he was the producer of the film and he goes around speaking, primarily in Texas. So we sit down, and the first question I ask him was, "So why did you leave the Church?" And he said, "Actually, I committed adultery, so I was excommunicated. I came back and after a couple of years, I decided to leave and have my name taken off the records."

So I look over at my Catholic mother sitting there—it was, like, adultery. I knew going in there that he wasn't going to tell me anything I didn't already know and that whatever he had to say was rubbish anyway. So my objective for going was to prove to my mom that this anti authority just couldn't hold water—my goal was just, you know, to discredit his authority in the eyes of my mother. And so the next question I asked him was, "Well, what church do you belong to now?" And he said, "Well, I sometimes go to the Methodist church, sometimes go to this Baptist church." So again, he is kind of like this homeless person as far as church goes. So then we proceed to talk a lot—it ended up being five hours—but at every point, you know, there are many more parallels between Mormonism and Catholicism than there are between Mormonism and Fundamentalism and between Catholicism and Fundamentalism. Like you have to be baptized with water—well, my mom and I agree on that. You know, there is priesthood authority— my mom and I agree on that. There are certain rites or performances or actions or sacraments, as they call them in Catholicism, that you have to do—we agree on that. Faith and works, we agree on that. And so slowly my mom began to realize that there are more similarities between us than there are differences. Granted, there are some very key differences, but there are more similarities than differences. And after five hours, he gets up to get a drink of water, and my mom said, "Can we please get out of here? I can't stand being here with this man."

So we left and I kind of left feeling like, "Mission accomplished." Like I just talked for five hours with this guy and kind of felt proud of myself, like I totally held my own with him, like I had an answer for everything he could come up with. I was excited about everything I had just learned, and I wanted to stand up for it.

I remember after my baptism, that day was awesome. The missionary who baptized me is Elder Johnson. Afterwards, I went home, I was by myself, and I just remember feeling like I was floating. I didn't want to do anything, you know, because I felt complete.

missionaries ride the bus
barcelona, spain

missionaries being rejected by someone who had been taking lessons about the church
stockholm, sweden

missionaries prepare lunch in their apartment
barcelona, spain

missionaries visit the metropolitan museum of art during their preparation day
new york, new york

during a going-away party for a missionary couple, the branch gives them a cake
brooklyn, new york

david kisses jessica outside their ward meetinghouse in stockholm
stockholm, sweden

DAVID AND JESSICA
stockholm, sweden
jessica converted to the church

JESSICA: When I was younger, I always had a sort of faith; I believed in something higher, but it was quite loose at the edges. And I felt that a lot of the examples that I had seen throughout the world had shown some bad sides of religion. So I felt that I wanted to just have my own perspective of things and believe in a higher being without it being organized.

DAVID: And there's a lot of bad stories in small societies in Sweden where the local sects were just crazy.

JESSICA: But I didn't think the Mormons were a sect or anything like that. I was very respectful of David and his beliefs, but I just felt that I couldn't go into the organized form because I didn't understand back then how it could actually help so much in your spiritual development, because I thought I could do that all on my own. And so that's why I took some time.

DAVID: But we started to translate the concepts into her language in a way, if you know what I mean. Well, for example, a couple of words, Swedish people don't really associate the positive things to the positive meaning we have in church for those words. So we just started to talk about those things.

JESSICA: More neutral.

DAVID: Yeah, and in a way we have a lot of analogies: it's like this, and it's like this. We explained it slowly and in a good way.

JESSICA: And David is great at explaining the principles in a completely understandable way so you just see the logic in it and you see the good things about it. It becomes nonfrightening, nonthreatening, and it just becomes, like, "Oh yeah, of course, when you say it like that I have to agree with you." But I guess some of the words have been so loaded when you are not a part of an organized church beforehand. A lot of Swedish people feel that way when you talk about sins and when you talk about being saved, because this is a secularized country. You don't feel that you need to be saved in Sweden because you think, "I'm not a sinner. I'm quite a decent person." So we haven't been taught what sin is. You get the idea that you have to be really bad.

DAVID: Exactly. You don't really know how to take it, like we shouldn't see the worst like that. So people get the cold shoulder often in Sweden.

JESSICA: I was very happy that the members were so warm.

DAVID: But you were afraid at first.

JESSICA: Yeah, I was a bit afraid.

DAVID: Nervous.

JESSICA: That was also the case, since I knew that David had been dating some girls before we started dating. I only came to the church after I left another relationship, and we got together and we'd been together for a while. I was a bit scared because I knew I was going to meet the other girls that had been interested in David before we got together. But it was a good thing because I was focused on my best behavior. There were some nice speeches the first time I went to church. During some parts I felt, "Oh, this is nice," and then some parts were a bit awkward because they were talking about sins and sinning and saying, "Be baptized, be saved." "Righteous" was also a difficult word, as if some people being in organized religion had some sort of opinion that they were better than others and that they looked down on people who were not in touch with God.

interview with david and jessica
stockholm, sweden

DAVID: Being a missionary, I experienced that a lot. People got the feeling that we thought we were better than them.

JESSICA: I went to church throughout the summer.

DAVID: In my case, it was an interesting period for me because I was praying a lot about getting married. I was praying a lot about this relationship and the road I should take. I felt so strong that Jessica was the one or the spiritual relationship that we had and that we had developed was very, very good. Actually one of the feelings I got very strongly in the beginning of our relationship was that, when I prayed, God felt that Jessica could give me a lot and I could give her a lot. We would have a great exchange—even though she wasn't a member yet—when it came to spiritual things.

JESSICA: Yeah, and I had had a lot of spiritual experiences before I met David when I just had this kind of loose faith, I don't know how to describe it. But when I started to open up to the possibility that we could actually believe in the same thing and that the Church might actually be a good thing, I started to get more intensified experiences and feel the presence of God in a different way than I had done before—more directly talking to me so that I could understand it. It wasn't a whole bunch of spooky feelings; it was clear and distinct.

DAVID: Yeah, when we talked about the gospel, we had wonderful spiritual experiences before we even got together.

JESSICA: When I, throughout the summer, went to church, I felt more and more of the Holy Spirit and more and more of God's presence, and we started reading the Book of Mormon.

DAVID: Yeah, we read the Book of Mormon together.

JESSICA: And we started praying a lot together. As I welcomed it more and more and got more sort of relaxed, I let down my guard and I didn't have to be so defensive.

DAVID: I actually asked Jessica if she could help me with my routines and my habits of reading and praying. Because if she didn't do it, it would be harder for me being in a relationship. So she did. And it was like everything unfolded, and we started going to this ward.

JESSICA: We were married then.

DAVID: Yeah, we were married then.

JESSICA: We got married in September, and then you moved to me in Jakobsberg, and then we started going to that ward. And then I got more included, because before we had been to church, and I had not been so involved. I'd been meeting a lot of lovely people, but it wasn't as included in my life as when we went to Jakobsberg Ward.

DAVID: No, this time, she got a sort of calling even though she wasn't a member yet. So I became the president of the activities committee, and Jessica had an activity every week: Pilates every Saturday. So a lot of women in church came to that.

JESSICA: And men.

DAVID: And men, yes. And men.

JESSICA: And then we did some parties like Halloween and Christmas.

DAVID: We helped with decorating and with the parties. We helped out a lot in the ward together. It's a small ward, and we became good friends with the bishop, who is twenty-eight, not much older than us, and then the first counselor.

JESSICA: And because we were quite engaged in those activities and I was praying a lot and we were reading a lot, I understood more and more. It all started to open up. And then I prayed a lot. And, then I went to church, even when David was sick, so I started being more…

DAVID: That was actually the time you decided to…

JESSICA: Yeah, I sort of got it. I realized, "OK, I need this." There was one thing that I needed before I decided completely. I could see that I had accepted the Book of Mormon, and I had accepted that Joseph Smith was the prophet and all the other basic things that you have to understand. But I still felt that I didn't really have a relationship with Jesus Christ. I only had a relationship with my Heavenly Father, and I could feel the Holy Spirit, and I could develop spiritually by going to church. But I didn't feel Jesus Christ sort of near me, him understanding me and me completely understanding who he was. So I prayed for that, to get a testimony of him when I got home one day, and I got his answer, and that is my testimony: about him telling me that he had been waiting for me. I could almost see him, and it was

interview with david and jessica
stockholm, sweden

a very strong spiritual experience. That was the last bit of the puzzle that I needed.

DAVID: You were like super happy and you said, "You know what? I want to get baptized now."

JESSICA: Before that I had been sort of feeling that I knew I was going to, because there was a period that I was thinking, "OK, because my love for David is so strong, I have to get baptized or this won't work." I would have done it because of that. And when I started thinking that…

DAVID: But I didn't want…

JESSICA: I've never felt any pressure in the least from David. So I had that period for a while. Then I had a period where I kind of understood, "Oh, I think I'm actually going to get baptized one day." I got some answer from God, that you are doing some good things now as a nonmember, so it's not right just now. So I was like, OK, and I just continued doing that.

DAVID: It's like you were being a better missionary for friends if you weren't a member yet, or something.

JESSICA: And I felt the other way around as well, that it was good.

DAVID: It's like people make a difference to people outside and inside church, a big difference. So I think it's good for people in church to socialize more with nonmembers and get to know them and understand they're spiritual beings as well and know that they are children of our Heavenly Father.

JESSICA: I didn't know how long that period was supposed to be. So I just waited for another answer to know the time to get baptized. And that is when I got the answer from Jesus as well and my Heavenly Father sort of said to me, "Now go and do it." It was very intense. I was shaky. I got the blessing…

DAVID: The gift of the Holy Ghost, the same day.

JESSICA: And during the time before my baptism, I talked to the missionaries, they were a big part of it. It was two girls in Jakobsberg. They were good support. I was very happy before as well, but now I'm happier in a different way. I have my ups and downs, but I always feel that I have a better tool to get on the right track. So I can shift from a bad mood to a good mood much quicker and better.

I was living in a nonspiritual mode before and I wanted more spiritual experiences but couldn't find them.

DAVID: She wanted it.

JESSICA: I wanted it.

DAVID: Hunger and thirst.

We talk about our spirituality a lot. We have a lot of friends that are not members of the church. And we have dinner, and there are a lot of spiritual discussions. So it's a big part of our lives to have spiritual discussions with people.

JESSICA: Yeah, beforehand, I wanted more spirituality in my life, but I had maybe one or two friends that I could talk with. And now it's just like every person I know who are not members are open to talking about God and prayer. They are just thrown at me, so I am very blessed and happy about the opportunity that I get to talk about God all the time.

DAVID: We pray a lot too. We read the scriptures, ten pages for the day.

JESSICA: It's really good, and it affects our home in a great way.

DAVID: Yeah, everyone that comes into our home, they get very calm. And they always say, "It's such a nice atmosphere here." And it's really cool because we had intended that atmosphere. We've always prayed that we would have a good spirit at home.

The Church is true.

JESSICA: The Church is true.

I'm just very happy to have found this spot. I feel very content now. A lot calmer and happier in a deeper sense.

general conference
salt lake city, utah

PERFECTING THE SAINTS

two young mormon men wait outside for general conference
salt lake city, utah

"we're from nevada—in our town everyone wears a flat-brimmed hat; it's kind of our thing."

john bicycles to visit people in his ward
provo, utah

JOHN
provo, utah
bishop

I've been involved in some difficult things as a bishop: deaths in families and difficulties in marriages, just a lot of things that are stressful for me and stressful for them. It's not like I've wanted to have to hear the darker side of individual lives. But when they then turn around and make great strides in their personal life in a positive direction, then that's good.

You have to have people that are willing to make changes. You kind of feel like you want everybody to be as happy as they can. So you try whatever you need to do and hope it will bless their life and make them happier and that they'll be better as a result of it. And sometimes when they don't accept or can't quite grasp that, then it's kind of hurtful to you—you maybe feel like you've failed a little. I don't look back with any regret. I mean, there are some things that I could have done differently or done better. But I feel good about what I've been able to assist people with. I haven't done anything great or wonderful, you know, but what has happened has been pretty meaningful to the people it's affected. It's not worthy of the front page or any great thing. But that's the way of the Church, you know—the Church quietly goes about helping each other and strengthening each other, being good neighbors and friends.

John helps a member of his ward
provo, utah

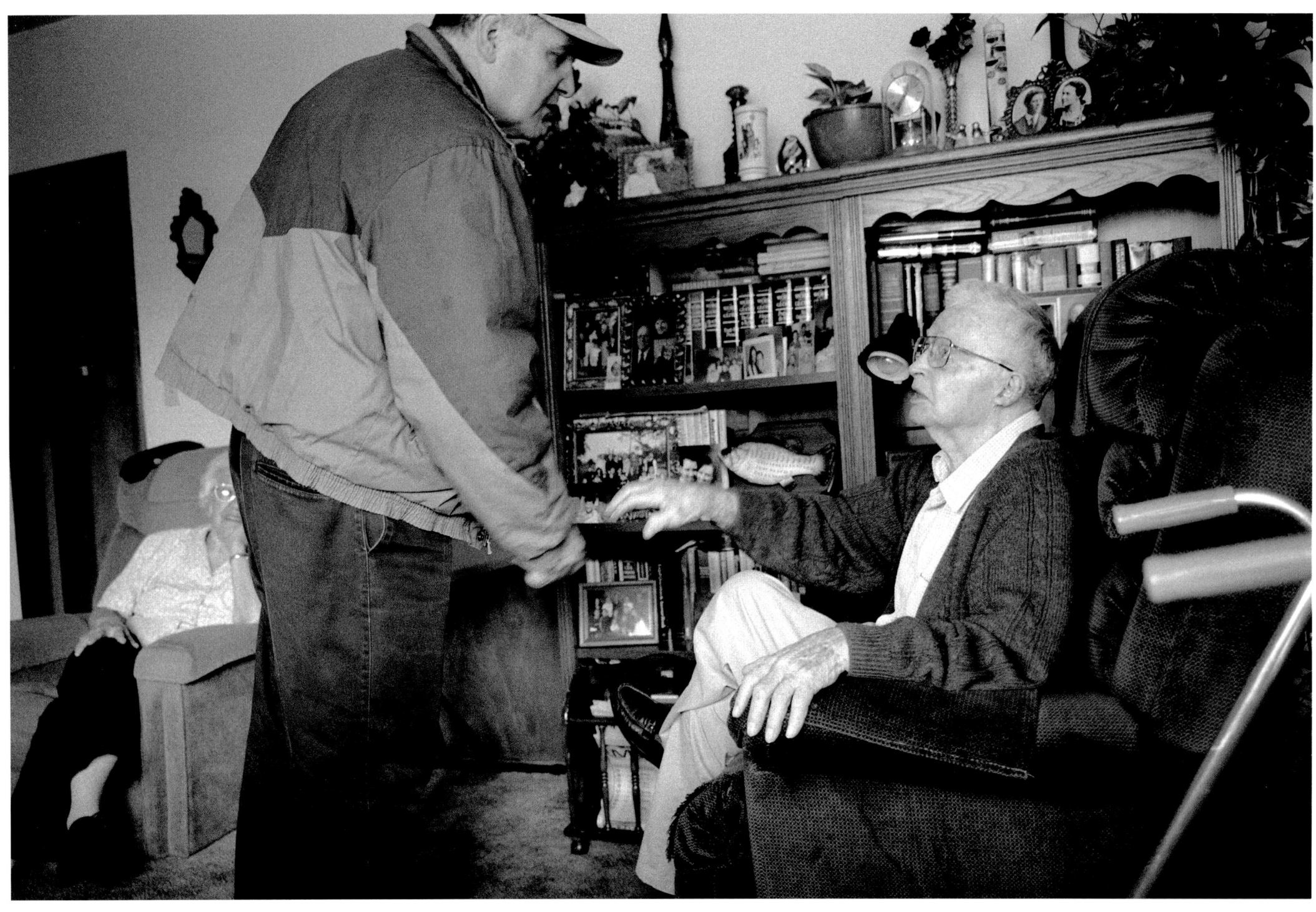

a young single adult group reacts to a once- or twice-a-year rainstorm
cairo, egypt

prayer during primary
brooklyn, new york

baby strollers in the church foyer
stockholm, sweden

primary song posters used in a sacrament meeting program
brooklyn, new york

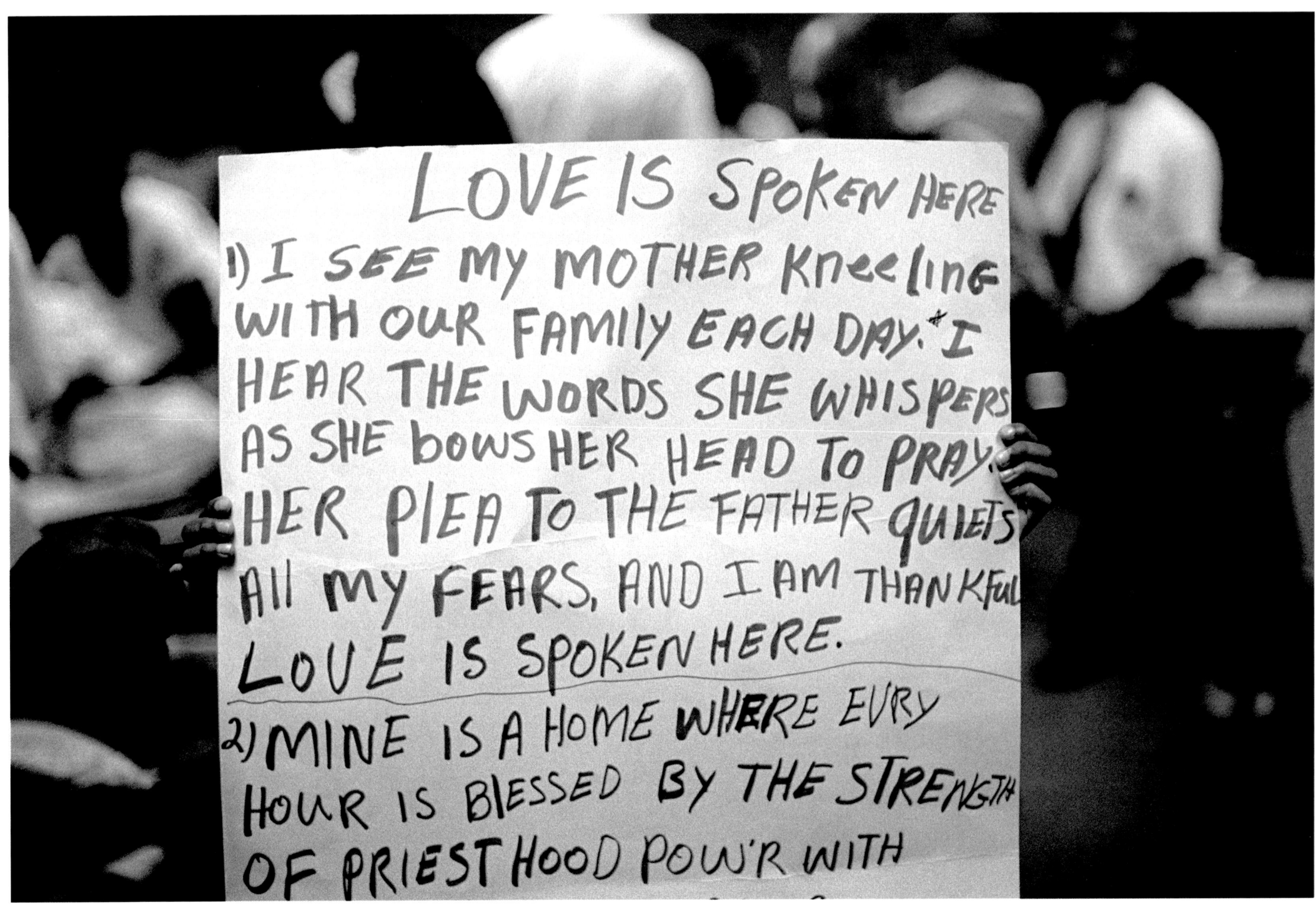

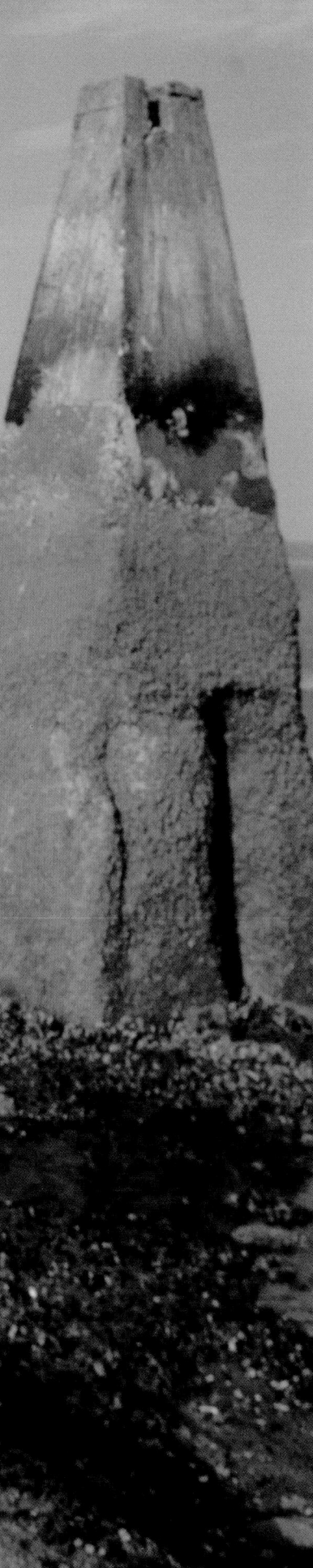

jessica with her daughter
edinburgh, scotland

JESSICA
edinburgh, scotland
member

Bishop McLaughlin was an incredible bishop and home teacher—pretty selfless, very giving of his time, and very understanding in a way that was totally, wholly appropriate and spiritual, and he was on the phone if I ever needed him. He would call me regularly and do home teacher visits and blessings. And if he couldn't come, he would send someone who he could trust with a blessing for me. He sorted out my finances—got me out of debt by arranging a debt-free program. I am now out of debt. I will never go back into debt because he taught me how miserable I was when I was in debt. I never want to go back to that. He taught me how to live within my means. He taught me how to deal with conflict. He has taught me how to have confidence in myself.

But, most of all, he taught me these things through prayer, scripture study, and being constant in my Church callings. Then everything he taught me about the gospel has come to fruition. I see it. It's reaffirmed for me that he was right because it has actually come true, whatever he taught. He was an immense help. I don't think I would have stayed a member without his help and guidance.

bishop mclaughlin and his family
glasgow, scotland

mormon women outside the ghana temple
accra, ghana

79

a child celebrates getting an apple as part of a primary class lesson
brooklyn, new york

marie, a primary president, is hugged by her son while she is giving a lesson
brooklyn, new york

MARIE
brooklyn, new york
primary president

I'm from Haiti. I have lived in Brooklyn for about fifteen years. My calling as Primary president is important to me because I love children and I love teaching and I think, for the kids, it's really a start in the gospel—that's why it's important. The number one thing is that the children can always turn to me. If they know that someone loves them, they know that they will be all right, so there are a lot of things I teach them.

I come with my neighbors' kids because their mothers don't want to come to church. Sometimes these children feel lost at home. One time I remember I told them, "Your Heavenly Father loves you," and one little boy said, "He does?" And I was shocked. I said, "Everybody knows that." They can't believe their Father loves them, you know. That's something I know. You should have seen that glow in the little boy's eyes, knowing that somebody loves him.

My favorite thing is the games that I play with them. Once I was teaching the children about how my body is a temple. I said, "I have a garbage can, and you have your body, and then all the bad stuff, like cigarettes, beer—everything bad—you have to put in the garbage." And then they actually remember that 'cause my little son says, "Mommy, cigarettes goes in the garbage, right. Beer goes in there, things like that." I love playing these kinds of games with them. If they see it, they see the garbage picture and know that what is no good is going in the garbage, and all the good stuff goes in the body.

My favorite moment is when a child bears their testimony. Especially when it is one of the kids that is about five. I really feel good. I feel pleased too, you know, for a little child telling me how they felt when they got baptized. It was very touching. Because they are just new to the Church. They love being baptized, and they are accepted in the gospel, and we respect them for taking that choice.

I learn a lot, that's for sure. I learn to be a parent and how to be patient. So whatever I am doing in Primary, I try to take it home and practice it with my boys. I have four boys, ages five, four, three, and two.

To be honest, I don't think it's a hardship to be in Primary. One day there was a lady who said, "You have four kids at home, and your calling is Primary. Don't you get tired to come here and have to deal with all the kids?" It struck me the wrong way 'cause for her to talk about children like that, I feel like it's wrong, because I love kids and I don't feel like I'm coming to deal with people's kids, I'm coming here to teach them about their Heavenly Father and to help them. I don't think there's anything hard about Primary. Everything is set down. They have a manual, it's fun playing with the children, they sit down and listen, and it's fine with me. I don't think it's hard at all.

I do bribe the children a lot. They love to sing, so I play songs to them and do games with them. Little kids don't have to be there; they could stay home and sleep late. But, you know, they're making the effort to come. I find that very unique and humbling.

I joined the Church because I had a best friend who wanted to visit me. On Sunday they went to church, and she asked me to come along. I was eighteen years old.

My husband helps me a lot, 'cause the way we do it, he gets home— I'm home during the day with the kids—and when he gets home I'll leave and go to school. Then we just rotate. And then when he's off work, we have our little house. We get together and go to church and are very, very happy. He's my kids' role model; they love to see Daddy at church. Sometimes it's tough because my husband works. But I know my job and what I have to do, and I do it.

mormon young single adults watch a band play during a dance
stockholm, sweden

a display used during a sunday school lesson
paris, france

JEAN-CLAUDE
paris, france
bishop

I have been a member of The Church of Jesus Christ of Latter-day Saints since I was fourteen years old. I have worked and served in many different callings, and I was never searching to be a bishop, but one day, after my mission with my wife in 2002, the stake president called me, and he had an interview with me. I had a feeling that there would be something heavy. So weeks later I had another interview with the stake president, and he said to me, "OK, first I have to have an interview with your wife and then with you." Then he presented me with the calling. He was asking me, would I like to do it. And I was very, very, very touched, naturally, because it comes from the heavens. I didn't expect it.

I was a dancer. I was a ballet dancer for twelve years, and I worked very hard, then I started to learn jazz. Before I became a member of the Church, I didn't dance anymore professionally, and I was acting. I was working in an agency for the spectacular, for the fashion shows here in Paris. I did work with this group for nearly twelve years, and then I stopped. I was sixty so I decided to retire. I'm now using my time doing things for the Church: ballet for the Church for the talent evening, every kind of spectacular here in the Church. Lately I did a spectacular for conference with the young adults.

I haven't worked in my life as much as now. My head is only occupied with the things in the ward and the many things I do. From the morning until the evening, I am always mentally occupied with this service. But I find much satisfaction and much enjoyment in this calling. I think everything relies on love, you know—to love your fellowman and to see that Jesus is the Son of God and that he is what every one of us is aiming towards.

I can tell you I have lots of practice because of this calling. I can really feel many things that I didn't feel before about the needs of other people, especially members of our ward. I appreciate them, and I try to help them like each was my brother or sister. Sometimes people will come to see me because of a transgression, and even before they start, I get the feeling what's going on. Even before I was set apart as bishop, I was able to feel things in my heart, like how I knew about getting the calling. So usually when I prepare the things for the every-week meetings in church, I can really feel what I need to do.

For six months we didn't have a secretary here in the bishopric, and so I was really everywhere trying to get everything together. I would wake up during the week, and I would say a prayer in bed, and then I could feel in my soul what I had to do for the next week. I can testify that it comes from the Holy Ghost. And then when we have to decide something very quickly, I just say the things. I think this is the inspiration; this is what I need.

An example to me I have in my calling here in our stake is the stake president. Before he became a stake president, he was in the bishopric as the first counselor. And I was always very impressed by his actions, saying things and knowing. Watching the conference of the Church is also an inspiration. I'm always impressed by the Apostles and President Hinckley. Last year he came to Paris. We had a conference in the upstairs of a hotel, and they asked me to sit behind the rows of chairs where the Apostles and their wives were sitting. When President Hinckley came in, we were all naturally standing up, and he was about two inches from me. I can say I felt that he was really the President of the Church, that he was the man who was set apart because Jesus Christ called him to be prophet in this day.

Also I expressed my testimony just the next week after this conference, saying the same thing. Everyone felt the Spirit really strong. I was never searching for this, because I believed it, but now I can say I comprehend really that President Hinckley is a prophet of God.

jean-claude (right) confers with one of his counselors
paris, france

women in relief society repair clothing for orphans
accra, ghana

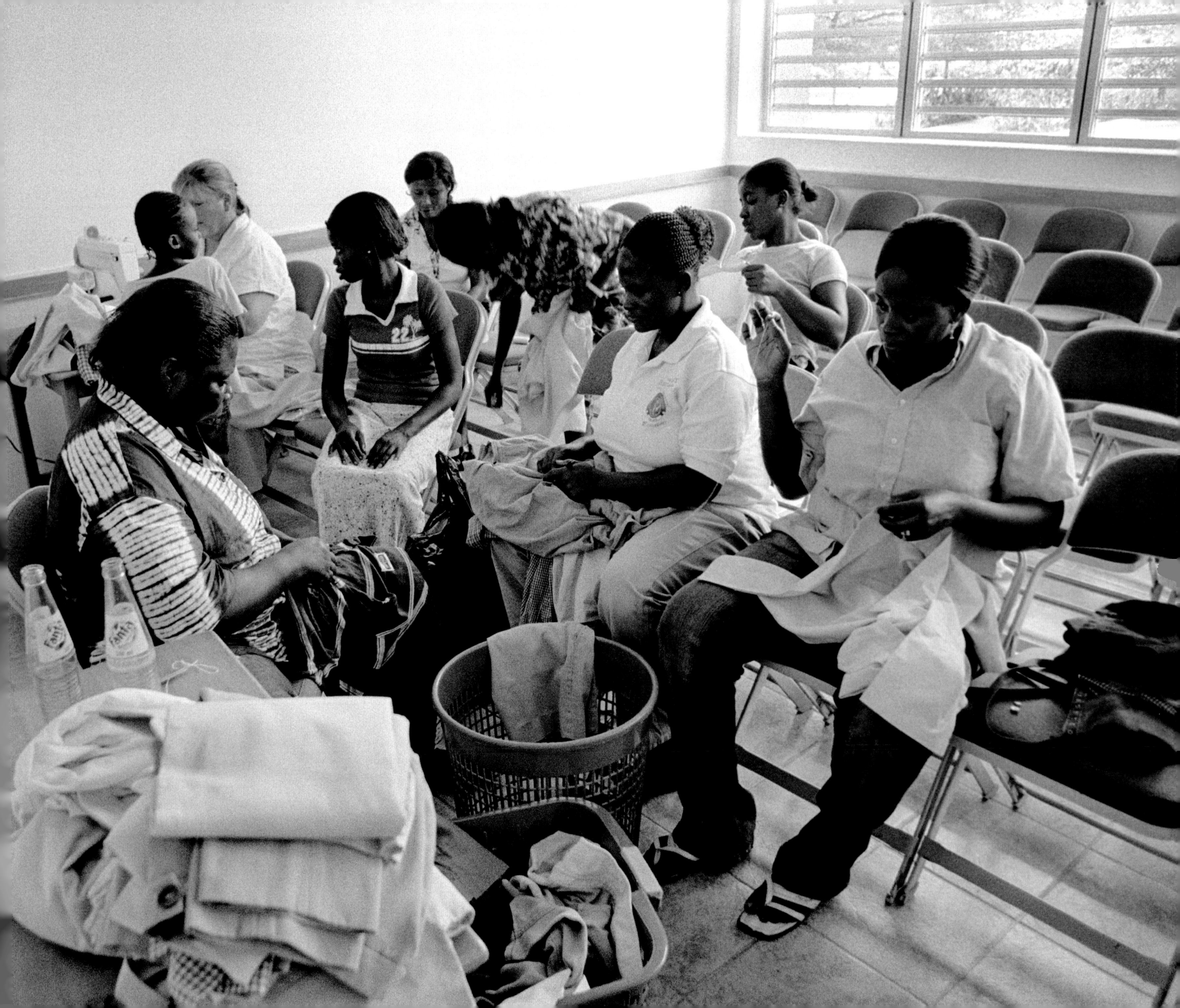

two mormon children read the *friend*
salt lake city, utah

baptismal clothes hung out to dry
accra, ghana

two mormon elders demonstrate how to perform a baptism
accra, ghana

helen plays a board game during a young adult family home evening activity
stockholm, sweden

HELEN
stockholm, sweden
young adult f.h.e. coordinator

My calling is great. Meeting people is cool because they have the same beliefs as me, and it's good to be with people that believe the same thing because it's just easier. And I get strength from them, and hopefully they will get something from me too.

My calling has been important because I have got to meet lots of people. I haven't been to church much in the last seven years. I knew people back then, but when I started coming back I didn't know them. So I got a chance to get to know everyone a lot better. For me that was perfect. So that was the best thing, I think.

The planning was awful, I must admit. It's just that every week I had to send out this e-mail to everyone because, you see, we have a mailing list, and that gets out to all the people, even people that don't come to church very often. I just had to plan early because I had to get this e-mail out, and then I didn't know if it was going to be sunny or rainy— we were outside during the whole summer. So I was glad every time we had sun because I would get to stay outside and do some sports.

My favorite sports are volleyball and soccer. We had a couple of missionaries that tried to teach us baseball, and it didn't go very well. Swedish people are not that great at baseball. So we did lots of volleyball, and we had a barbecue once.

But we had lots and lots and lots of activities, and investigators came. I was amazed. One of the reasons we have so many activities is to baptize more people and to get people to come back to church. Outreach is a program that we have in Europe because the growth is not that big here. So now they give lots of money and effort to the young adults, and there's just lots of activities, and the missionaries bring people.

My calling is not a big deal. I like having a calling that keeps me around all the young adults because I love being a boss over people to tell them what to do. I learned that I need to listen to people and I can't just "drive over them," as we say in Swedish. That's the thing that I can take with me from that time, that I have to listen to people a little bit more.

What are my future callings? I think that I will be a help, at least that's what it says in my patriarchal blessing. In it, it talks about my future callings and that I will be a help for young people, and so I hope that I can help them.

Maybe I can help them to understand that it's OK to come back to church after you have done lots of stupid things, because some people think, "Oh no, I did this. I can't come back."

I mean you get blessings for having a calling and doing your things, and I guess the family gets blessings for it too. But they don't know— they don't live here.

My family had five kids. And I grew up in the Church. All of my family are members in the Church, and I have an older sister that is married, and she has a girl that's the cutest one ever.

I just finished the University KTH as a chemical engineer, and now I'm taking another year to study environmental security and health security.

a sunday school lesson
accra, ghana

a prayer is given before a baptism
cape coast, ghana

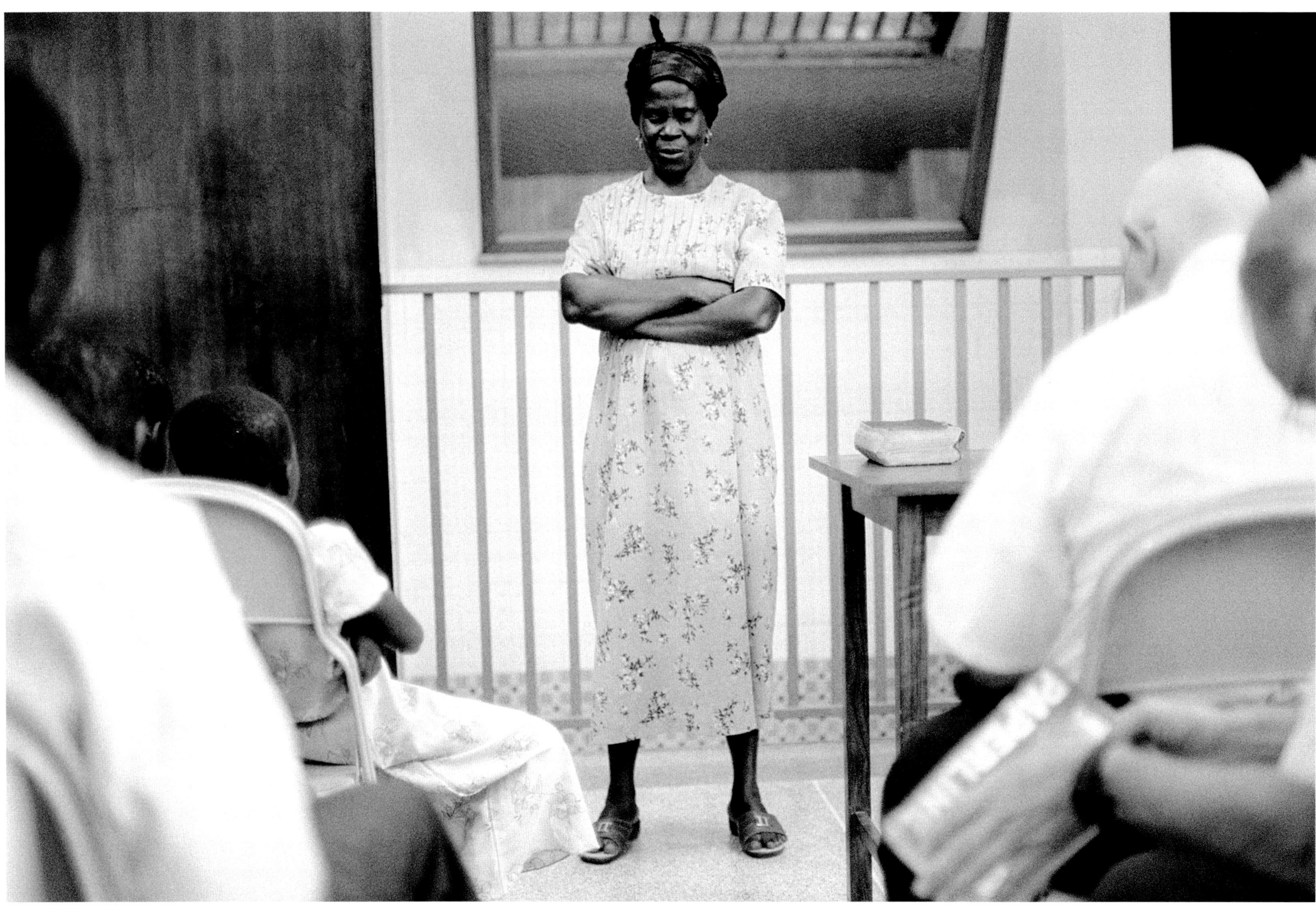

people listening to general conference outside on temple square
salt lake city, utah

a woman leads the ward in singing a hymn during sacrament meeting
paris, france

two boys play in the foyer after church
paris, france

a young women leader walks to class with her girls
paris, france

young mormon mother of two outside the library
st george, utah

a 'church of jesus christ of latter-day saints' sign on the side of the road
accra, ghana

MARU
cancun, mexico
sunday school teacher

I'm a member of The Church of Jesus Christ of Latter-day Saints, and my name is Maru. I have lived in Cancun for more than twenty years. Church, for me, is everything. I cannot imagine my life without the Church. I don't know how my life would be if I didn't know the gospel. I like to teach because when you teach you are learning. You're not learning from what you have to teach, but you learn from those whom you're teaching. That's the important thing. That's why I am enjoying my calling. Being a member of the Church is a way of living. It's a style of living. There are things that you know you have to do because you know that is the way you can be happy. It's more like a style of living for us, for my daughter and for me.

There's something that I always feel respect for. I admire seeing teenagers every Sunday in Sunday School and knowing that none of their family are members of the Church. Thirteen- and fourteen- and fifteen-year-old teenagers that go to church and their parents are not members of the Church—this is what makes my heart beat. I respect them. I admire them because no one told them to wake up, to get up and go to church. They did it because they want to live according to the commandments, according to what our Lord wants us to be.

That's what I admire.

maru with her daughter
cancun, mexico

two men during a sunday school lesson
cairo, egypt

109

an elders quorum
stockholm, sweden

a young boy with his father at church
stockholm, sweden

a high priests group lesson
stockholm, sweden

gösta, a stake president, talks with his daughter after church
stockholm, sweden

GÖSTA
stockholm, sweden
stake president

My daughter said, "I was so glad that Dad is stake president because of tough times. If he wasn't the stake president, people wouldn't pray to support us so much." So that is my courage. I've been blessed, both as a person and in my calling.

First, I'm actually a convert. I wasn't born in the Church. I have been on a mission. I was called as a stake president when I was thirty-eight years old, in Sweden. I have thought about what it takes to be a member in Sweden because people don't go to church in Sweden. You have to decide for yourselves that you have to go to church—you can't be lukewarm. Either you go to church or you don't go to church. You don't go to church to be social. The people here are very strong. The people who go to church are very strong. The young adults have to take great risks, and they are about to witness that this is how the people take great risks, by going to church and by choosing to be strong.

I have my wife, Christina, and four children: Avalena (23), Cole (23), Rita (19), and Steve (17). The two oldest have started university, and the next is finishing high school, and she will start in February. My son is about to start to serve his mission. The interesting thing is that he was called from Stockholm to go to Singapore.

One year, at Christmas, our family prayed that we could do some service for one person. We went out with the family and sang for a sister who lived a one-and-a-half-hour drive from our home. She started to cry, because she didn't have her own children there. She was very appreciative, and that felt really good. We have lots of members that have come back to the Church because of service and love that other members have shown them, and I see how they grow. That's what I really like.

In my calling, I think the hardest thing is actually to have disciplinary courts, even though it is a very spiritual thing. I can see why we have it. The people have problems; it's very tough. I'm glad to assist them. You feel love for them. I feel that the greatest problem is that people don't go to the Lord to say, "I have a problem with this. Can you help?" They need to be meek in their heart so they can listen to the Lord. But when they are hard-hearted and say, "I don't have any problems," they're hard on themselves, and their problems become worse. Then they're not helped, and then sometimes you have to have the disciplinary court.

The Lord has longer patience and sees a longer time. He sees that the people are purified and that they grow. I mean, he has patience and he sees the development of one person and the effect it has on future generations.

My view of time has totally changed. If I find two people that have been married in the temple and they need help, I can help them. I have the patience to help them. I know that I am helping them and their children and their grandchildren. I actually help generations.

suy, first counselor in a branch presidency, gives a member a church publication
phnom penh, cambodia

SUY
phnom penh, cambodia
first counselor

We can say everybody has a calling, and I have my responsibility. Even in the small jobs, I am in need of guidance a little. I need to pray all the time and do a little planning.

I enjoy serving no matter what calling I have. And it's real and Heavenly Father and Jesus Christ have a plan for everybody to participate in the Church.

We organize a home teaching program. The members of the branch have the families to go visit at their homes and teach. But I felt, you know, all members need to understand that we're not alone. They have people from the Church to support them.

The thing the members need is to understand that there is God to help them. If they have any problems with their life, you know, they can pray to him and ask him for direction. Many scriptures mention faith, also that if you ask you will receive. A lot of scriptures say that if you pray in faith God will help you. If all the members understood that, they would stay active.

In Cambodia in my branch there are a lot of challenges. First, the members join the Church; one year later they usually become less active. So then the branch prays for them and the elders pray. They need to work hard to have them to come back to the Church. Teaching how to help the people feel the Spirit, that's most important. That's my challenge.

captain lineback, chaplain in the united states navy, conducts a mormon church service
twenty-nine palms, california

playing a game during nursery class
provo, utah

the attendees of general conference leave the conference center
salt lake city, utah

carving pumpkins for a youth activity
provo, utah

a group eats lunch between sessions of a broadcast of general conference
glasgow, scotland

studying during sunday school
cancun, mexico

a float made by the orem latter-day saint institute of religion for the provo freedom festival
provo, utah

a man prays
brooklyn, new york

roth teaches a sunday school lesson
phnom penh, cambodia

ROTH
phnom penh, cambodia
sunday school teacher

My family escaped to Thailand during the war, and I was born there. I was twelve years old when I came back to Cambodia with my family. I joined the Church in 1996. At that time the Church was just set up in Cambodia. The missionaries did a class where they taught English; I went to study with my friend who also took discussions with the missionaries. She was about sixteen, and she was scared to sit with the missionaries alone. My friend asked, "Can you come with me? I know you don't want to become a member. Let's just sit together or something." So I just joined in with her. After the missionaries taught all the discussions, they were inviting my friend to get baptized. I just felt like I wanted to get baptized too. So I asked the missionaries if I could get baptized. They started teaching me the discussions again, and I was baptized.

My parents were baptized five months before I left for my mission in 2002, so they are pretty new to the Church too. It was really good for me because I had only been a member for four years when I went on my mission. When I got over there, I just felt like I learned more than I ever taught people.

I went on my mission to Fresno, California. The Church has been over there [in Fresno] for a long time. The people know everything in the Church already. But people here, they learn only by their heart, and they learn by their feelings. And some people don't even know how to read. But they come and sit in the class and listen to me. I feel like it's really special that I have this chance to help all these people. They always want to know more. They always want to know why this happened or why that happened.

I've been a Sunday School teacher since I got back from my mission. Teaching is my favorite thing to do. I'm teaching, but I don't feel that I'm a teacher. I just always tell people in my class that I am a member just like all of you. We just want to share something together. I don't have a bachelor's degree in teaching, so we need to learn from each other. Sometimes I feel like I don't know enough to answer all their questions, but I follow the Spirit to try to help them understand the purpose of life.

I also help with the young adults. People in Cambodia don't date; our parents arrange marriages. Some people date in a group, but some do not. It's hard, you know, when people become members of the Church and then marry outside the Church. It's kind of like they fall or part from the Church a little. This does not mean they are bad people. It's just hard. So I feel like the young adult activities are important. I feel like we bring the adults in the Church together, and we get to know each other and we share—we talk about the purpose of being married. We have Sister Towers—she teaches us about preparing for life. So we talk a lot about who we should marry and what kind of people we want to be. Then after that, we play together.

Since I joined the Church, I feel like our family got closer together. You know, before it was like my sister would do a different thing and my mother would do a different thing, but right now it's kind of like when we decide to go to church, when we decide to go to conference, we support each other. We have more fun and get closer together.

praying at the close of sunday school
moab, utah

rebecca with a pie she made to use as refreshments for her class
los alamos, new mexico

REBECCA
los alamos, new mexico
teacher development leader

I like to have refreshments when I teach. It's not the same as having a whole meal, but you feel like you are giving to people on a lot of levels, not just getting the job done. There are not a lot of other things I can do without being annoying. The teachers that I train don't want to hear four lessons a month. They want one lesson every three months. So I just try to make it memorable.

When I work on a lesson, first I go through all the things I wish I could talk about: the things I've prepared, the neat ideas, the "Wow! This will blow them over" kind of stuff. But most of the time [those ideas] all have an insubstantial feel to them. It takes a fair amount of time turning things over and thinking about the people. Then, usually when I'm not even thinking about it, the ideas come to me—the ideas that have that correct ring to them, like when you thump a watermelon and it sounds just right—and I know this is the thing I need to talk about.

A good lesson is if people go away saying, "I can do that. That is something I can do, and I see the way to do it." You can see it when people in class begin to flare up. They catch on. They start talking without raising their hands and talk to each other. That's annoying from a teacher's aspect, but it's very cheering when you genuinely see people begin to get it.

In connection to my calling, all the very best scriptures on teaching are in Doctrine and Covenants section 88. There's a very good one that talks about the ideal classroom, where the teacher is supposed to speak, then everyone is supposed to have an equal voice, all contributing and all benefiting.

This is section 88 of the Doctrine and Covenants, verse 122: "Appoint among yourselves a teacher, and let not all be spokesmen at once," which of course means "everyone shut up." "But let one speak at a time and let all listen unto his sayings, that when all have spoken that all may be edified of all, and that every man may have an equal privilege." And of course the very next verse says, "See that ye love one another; cease to be covetous; learn to impart one to another as the gospel requires."

That's what I would like all classrooms to be: where we all teach each other—until, of course, the time when the Lord will come, and then we won't need to teach each other about the Lord because everyone from the least to the greatest will know the Lord and be taught by him.

students from the brigham young university center for near eastern studies walk through the old city
jerusalem, israel

a church member cleans the meetinghouse
gunlock, utah

a stake basketball game
st. george, utah

a family gets ready to leave after a meeting in the st. george tabernacle
st. george, utah

a family arrives for church
toquerville, utah

elder jeffrey r. holland (an apostle) and his wife, patricia, and grandchildren greet a church member in a diner
st. george, utah

funeral
spanish fork, utah

REDEEMING THE DEAD

temple
vasterhaninge, sweden

lobby of the family history center
salt lake city, utah

cemetery
toquerville, utah

a mormon wedding party outside a temple
san diego, california

evan in the brigham young university family history library
provo, utah

EVAN
provo, utah
member

There are a lot of people in the world that aren't Church members that think there is no relation between temple work and family history, but to me it's everything. There are two sides to the coin to me. One side is that I'm something of a historian. I just love history. I was reading history books on ancient Europe to modern Europe to United States—you name it. I just love history. Then the other side of the coin is, of course, that we're trying to get the work done for our kindred and dead. My driving motivation in all cases is to find work that hasn't been done, as opposed to the work that's been done forty-seven times that you run into continually. I try to avoid that. The other part is, I like going to the temple.

What I like most about the temple is that it changes me. When I go and come back out, there's so much of the Spirit that some of it rubs off on me. I am a better person when I come out. I'm not always the greatest person, but I'm a better person than I would be and it's because I'm going to the temple twice a week, I assure you.

The more you go to the temple, the more you tend to overcome the breaking of the commandments that we're all trying to fight. Temple attendance helps me have charity, which I'm often lacking. It increases my faith, it increases my hope, and the more I've been to the temple, the more the Spirit is able to guide me in what I do, so I don't make quite so many stupid mistakes in life.

The more you go to the temple, the more you have an understanding of the bigger picture. The entire temple endowment ceremony gives you the big view, how here on this earth it's just a little piece of the whole thing. It's only been a few weeks since my mother died, and when my mother went, it was marvelous news because her body was old and worn out—done for. I felt only joy, no sadness because I knew exactly where she is. I didn't have to worry about her misery anymore when I say my prayers with my wife at night. I no longer have to mention my mother in my prayers because I'm not worried about her. She is in great shape now.

"god's plan of happiness" written outside a subway stop
new york, new york

a woman studies microfilm at the brigham young university family history center
provo, utah

students box up microfilm
provo, utah

three young women walk to the temple to do baptisms for the dead
st. george, utah

a woman exits the garden tomb
jerusalem, israel

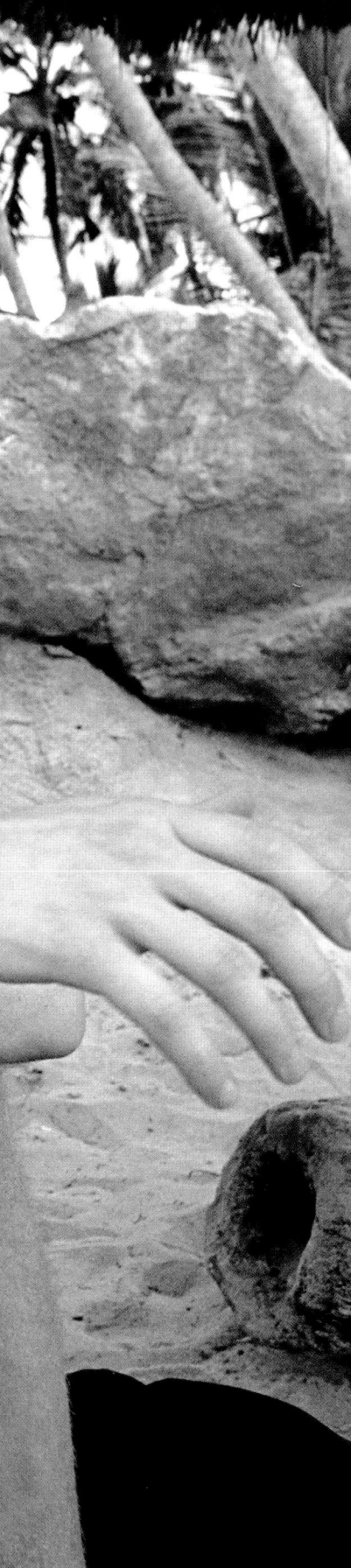

mark hedengren
ghana, west africa

AFTERWORD
mark hedengren

The Mormons took me five years to make, and it became a thread that tied my life together. For me to flip through its pages is to fast-forward through my life—the hard times and the good times. This book contains every moment I got off a plane and was awed by the climate, language, and people of an alien environment. It contains every time a taxi driver ripped me off.

In photographing this book I was deeply influenced by medieval art and early Mormon folk painting. I love the simplicity of gesture and movement in tapestries, stained glass, and frescoes of that time. I tried to mimic them as often as I could.

It is difficult to photograph Mormons in an honest way because it seems that no matter what you do, there are two camps that will get upset. One camp wants to see Mormons depicted only in a sort of superhuman wonderfulness: perfect beyond reality. The other camp wants to see them depicted only as evil, corrupt, stupid, silly, and a number of other demeaning things. I tried to ignore these two bodies and to depict Mormons for what they are—people.

The interviews add a human dimension because you get to listen to the photographs speak. You get to hear the subjects tell you their stories. I hope you have read them. In both the photographs and the interviews, I tried to keep my hand light. I feel that the people are interesting in their own right. To listen to the audio interviews and see additional content, go to www.themormonsthebook.com.

It is important to point out that Mormons have a volunteer clergy. The members of the congregation will serve without pay in various positions for a limited period of time. This means the people photographed in this book are clergy and members, all tied up into one. It means that when you walk into a Mormon church service, nobody has any financial interest in your being there.

When you photograph, you rely emotionally and sometimes physically on your subjects. They become your friends. I wish to thank everyone who allowed me to photograph and interview them and allowed me into their lives. It was a precious gift.

I feel the people who read books like this are a special breed. They are citizens who want to enlarge their world, who want to find out more about others. It's a very selfless attitude. Thank you for taking the time to look at this book.

END

GLOSSARY OF TERMS

APOSTLE: Member of the Quorum of the Twelve Apostles, one of the governing bodies of the Church.

BISHOP: Leader of a ward.

BRANCH: Smallest official congregation of Mormons.

BRANCH PRESIDENT: Leader of a branch.

COUNSELOR: Assistant to a bishop, stake president, or branch president.

DISTRICT MEETING: A meeting of about two to four pairs of missionaries.

ELDER: Formal title of a male missionary.

ELDERS QUORUM: All active men in the Mormon Church hold the priesthood and are members of either an elders quorum or a high priests quorum.

FAMILY HOME EVENING (F.H.E.): A time on Monday nights when a Mormon family studies the scriptures, plays games, or generally spends time together.

FRIEND, THE: Official magazine published by the Church with content aimed at children.

GENERAL CONFERENCE: A series of general church meetings held semiannually involving the entire Church. They are held in Salt Lake City and broadcast around the world.

HIGH PRIESTS QUORUM: Similar to the elders quorum except the men are generally older.

PRIMARY: Sunday School for children ages two to eleven.

PRIMARY PRESIDENT: Leader of the Primary.

RELIEF SOCIETY: All women eighteen and older in The Church of Jesus Christ of Latter-day Saints are members of the Relief Society.

RELIEF SOCIETY PRESIDENT: The head of the Relief Society in a ward.

SISTER: Formal title of a female missionary.

STAKE: A collection of about six to twelve wards.

TEMPLE: A sacred building where weddings and other ceremonies take place which have particular relevance to the afterlife.

WARD: A congregation of Church members.

YOUNG SINGLE ADULT: An unmarried member who is eighteen to thirty years of age.

YOUNG MEN: A program for boys ages twelve to seventeen.

YOUNG WOMEN: A program for girls ages twelve to seventeen.

ZONE CONFERENCE: A meeting of about twenty to sixty missionaries in a geographical area.

SPECIAL THANKS

I would like to thank Lynn Poulter (Provo High School), Dean Duncan (BYU), Merrill Webb (Provo High School), Pat Buckner (Dixon Middle School), and Francis McKee (Glasgow School of Art) for being excellent and influential teachers. I would also like to thank Tom Smart (*Deseret News*), Janet Hart and Brian Winter (*Daily Herald*), Brad Slade (BYU), Governor Michael Leavitt (State of Utah), and Lauren Greenfield for giving me jobs where I learned much of what I know about photography and the nature of work.

I'm also indebted to my friends David and Renea Janetski, Shelley Spencer, Tessa Clark, Marin Turley, Nathan Packard, Nate Keith, Caroline Welty, David Hobben, Anne Jensen, Karl-Johan Berggren, and Nathan Robison, who have helped me in many ways with their friendship and advice throughout my life. I also wish to thank my family—Mary, David, Emily, Anna, Paul, and Beth—who are my closest friends.

I can't express the gratitude I have for the people directly involved with the making of *The Mormons*. Chris Ramsey, Julie Williamsen, Tom Wells of the BYU Harold B. Lee Library, and Bridget Rees and Jamie Lawson of *LDS Living Magazine*. Without support and encouragement, I wouldn't have photographed *The Mormons*. I am indebted to Richard Neitzel Holzapfel. I also would like to thank Vikki Miller for her excellent graphic design work.